Conceived by Jean Saucet
Text by Sarane Alexandrian
Translated from the French by Eleanor Levieux

MAX ERNST

© Editions Filipacchi, 65, av. des Champs-Elysées,
Paris 8, and © by S.P.A.D.E.M., Paris, 1971. English text
© 1972 by J. Philip O'Hara, Inc.

All rights reserved. Nothing herein may be reproduced
in any form without written permission from the publisher.
Manufactured in Spain.

J. Philip O'Hara, Inc., 20 East Huron, Chicago 60611.
Published simultaneously in Canada by Van Nostrand Reinhold Ltd.,
Scarborough, Ontario.

Library of Congress Catalogue Card Number: 79-189277

ISBN: 0-879555-602-1

First printing A

A Howard Greenfeld Book
J. PHILIP O'HARA

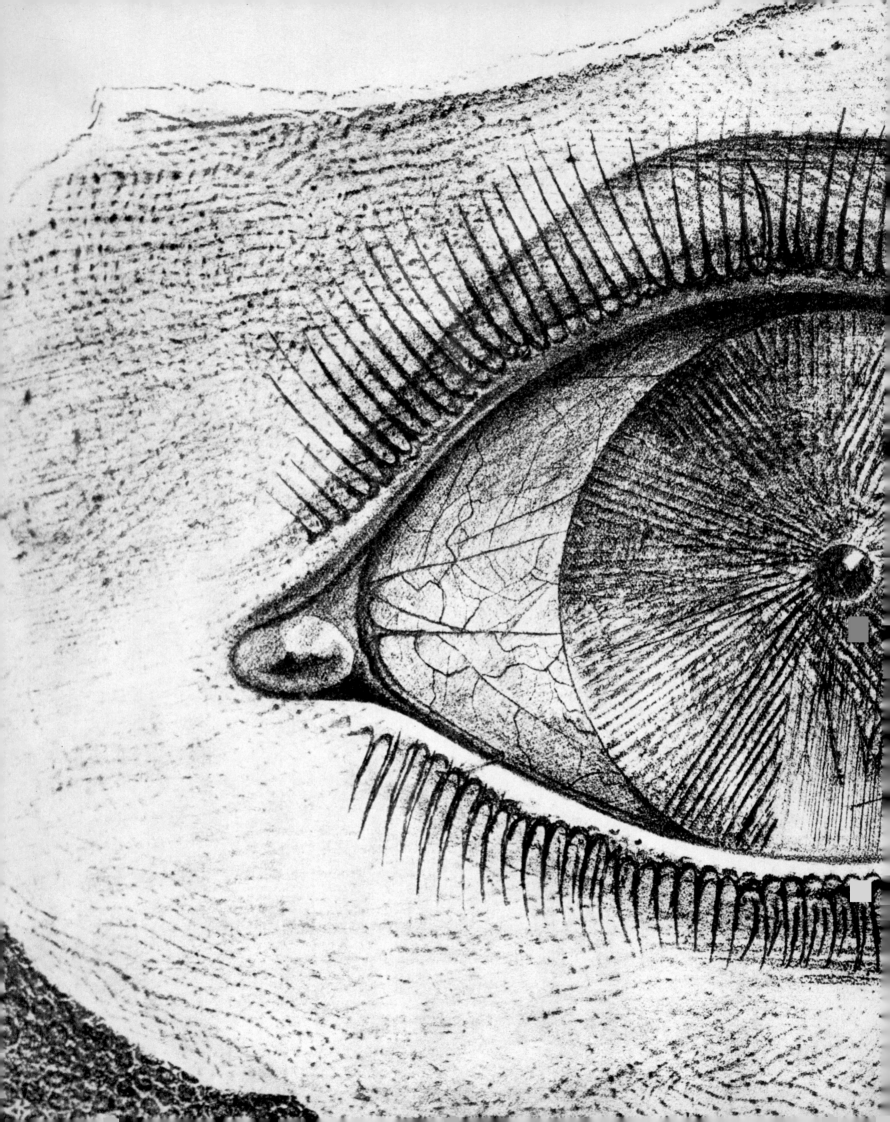

A GAME OF BOULES WITH

Max Ernst at the exhibition of his work in the Orangerie (Paris), April 2, 1971

On the limpid, early August day when I arrived in Huismes, in the French département of Indre-et-Loire, the man who used to style himself "Minimax Dadamax in person" was picking tufts of tarragon in his garden. After a hug and the traditional, welcoming glass of champagne, Max Ernst, faithful to a long-standing rite, suggested a game of boules. A game which occupies such an important place in his life that I have sometimes wondered whether the seriousness, the gravity with which he approaches it do not make up, to some extent, for the humor and fantasy distilled in his work.

PATRICK WALDBERG: A young man came to see me in Paris, named Ewald Rathke. He's organizing something in Düsseldorf...

They want to know. Dada is a unique phenomenon, still not clearly understood, not very well known...

Interesting from the historical standpoint, perhaps...

MAX ERNST *(annoyed):* I know, I know, a Dada show. Another one! But, what's the matter with them all? Why must they make a museum piece out of Dada? *(He aims, tosses, misses.)* Dada was a bomb. Now, can you imagine anybody trying to pick up the pieces nearly half a century after a bomb has exploded and gluing them back together so as to put them on display?

Concentrating, silent, we continue until the score is tied at seven all.

M. E.: What are they going to find out that they didn't already know? They'll be shown objects, collages, through which we expressed our disgust, our indignation, our revolt. They'll see nothing in them but a phase, a "stage", as they call it, in «the history of art»: exactly the opposite of what Dada was looking for. And they'd like me to write something about it? *(Very sharply):* I am not a historian!

For us in Cologne, in 1919, Dada was a moral reaction, above all. We intended to sabotage performances of a monarchistic and patriotic play called The Young King, which was insultingly stupid. A friend named Baargeld and I used to station ourselves at factory gates and hand out copies of our review, Der Ventilator. In our rage, we were aiming for nothing less than total subversion...

Just then a lucky toss brings me very close to the jack, giving me what should be an unbeatable edge. Tense-faced, his arms stretched out before him like a

PATRICK WALDBERG

The Montmartre Fair, 1923: André Breton, Robert Desnos, De'teil, Paul Eluard, Max Morise, Max Ernst, Simone Breton, Gala Eluard

sleepwalker's, Max Ernst aims carefully. Then he suddenly relaxes and, with a masterful gesture, makes his ball knock mine away and take its place. A perfect toss. It puts him ahead, 10 to 9, and whoever has 11 will win. We are approaching the end.

P. W.: What was the reason for such fury? Wasn't there a single ray of hope on the whole sinister horizon?

A fine little community but short-lived...

All in all, you were looking, for disgrace-and you reaped laurels!

M. E.: A horrible, senseless war had deprived us of five years of existence. All that we had been taught was just, beautiful and right collapsed before our eyes, amid ridicule and shame. My works at that time were not meant to be appealing; they were meant to make people howl!

Yes, there was one thing, an exciting thing too: the discovery that far from being the only ones of their kind, our reactions were actually receiving a brotherly echo on the "winners'" side. That in Paris, just as in Berlin or Cologne, in Zurich, youth was being moved by the same impulse to rise up against stupidity and hypocrisy...

It was a privilege for Dada to die young. At least it forged a few characters and launched some lasting friendships. And possibly it made a small crack in the wall of imbecility.

Max Ernst smiles. While we have been busy talking, he, mischievously, has placed the jack on a slope so that the weight of the balls pulls them down into a little ditch. Mine roll down and are irremediably lost. But he knows his terrain. Using a skilful twist he puts his last ball a bare inch or two from the goal and so takes the decisive point. As usual, Max Ernst has won the game. He opens a second bottle. I, philosophically, refuse to think I've lost. After all, hasn't it been granted to me to share a poet's game and to bring forth these statements from his mouth, like quicksilvery little fish wriggling as they are lifted out of the currents of a great river?

Imst (Tyrol), 1921
Tristan Tzara, Maya Chruseces, Lou Ernst,
André Breton, Max Ernst

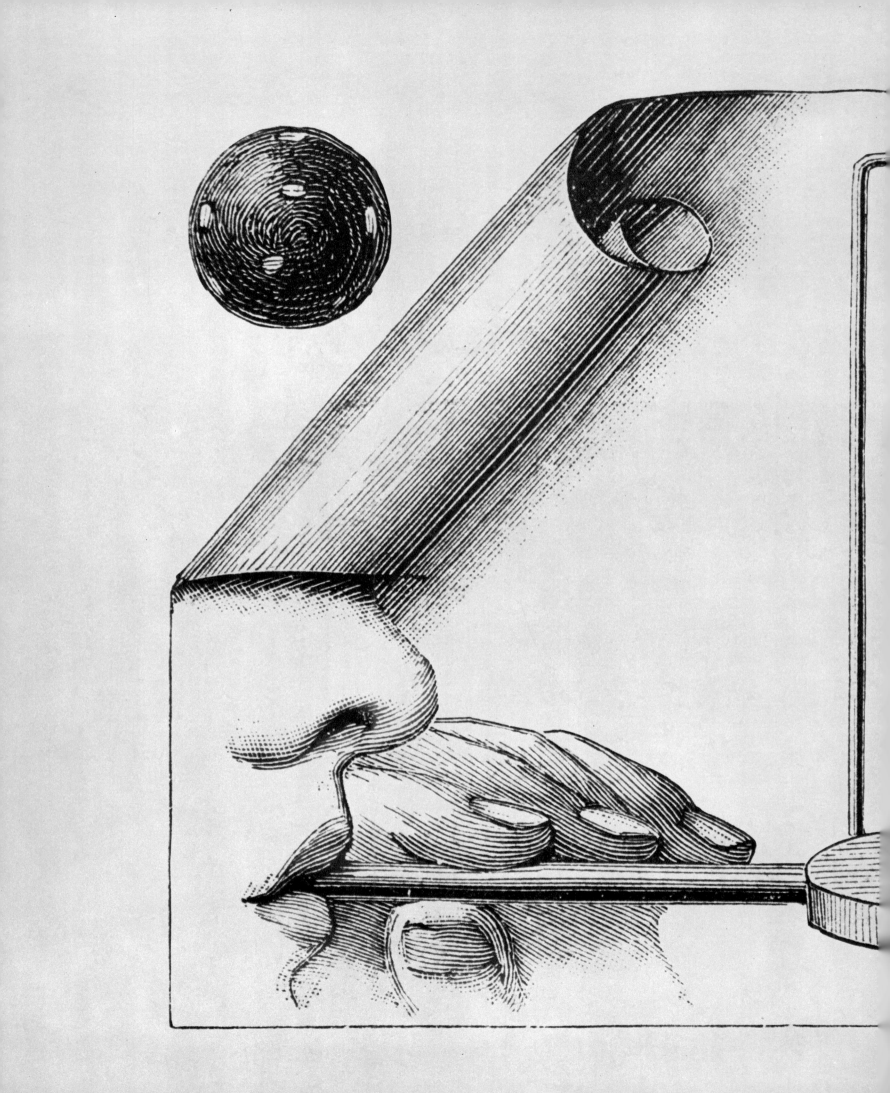

DIZZINESS AND DEFIANCE

The Virgin spanking the Infant Jesus before three witnesses: A.B., P.E., and the artist, 1926
78×52

Bird in cage, 1927
13.6 × 10

Gratenwald, 1927
(Fishbone Forest)
40 × 32.4

18

The birds that cannot fly
27 × 21.3

Following two-page illustration:
Weib, Greis und Blume, 1923-24 (Woman, Old Man and Flower)
38.6 × 52 (detail)

19

Domestic angel, 1935
15.2 × 18.4

Die Windsbraut, 1926-27
(Bride of the Wind)
32.4 × 40

Moon and Mars, 1946
15.8 × 18.4

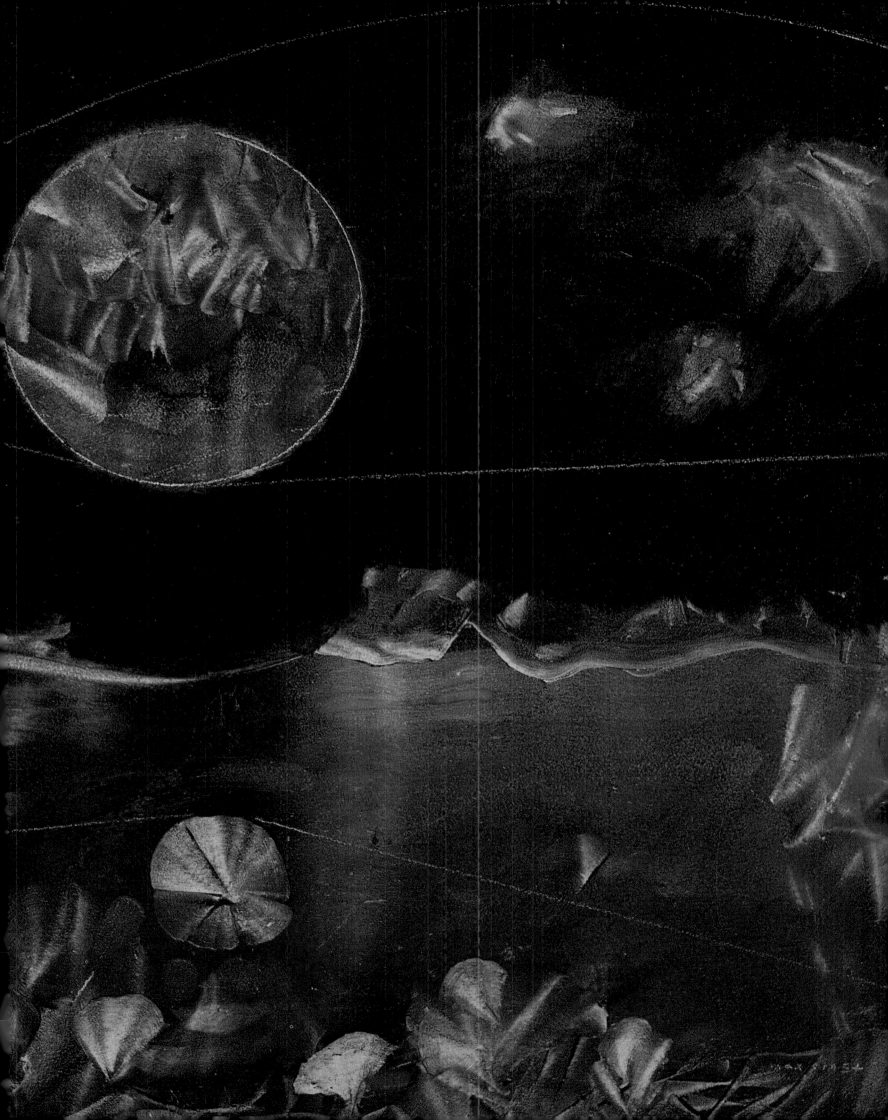

Le déjeuner sur l'herbe, 1935-36
18.4 × 22

26

Man's head, 1934
29.2 × 24

27

Europe after the rain, 1940-42
21.8 × 59

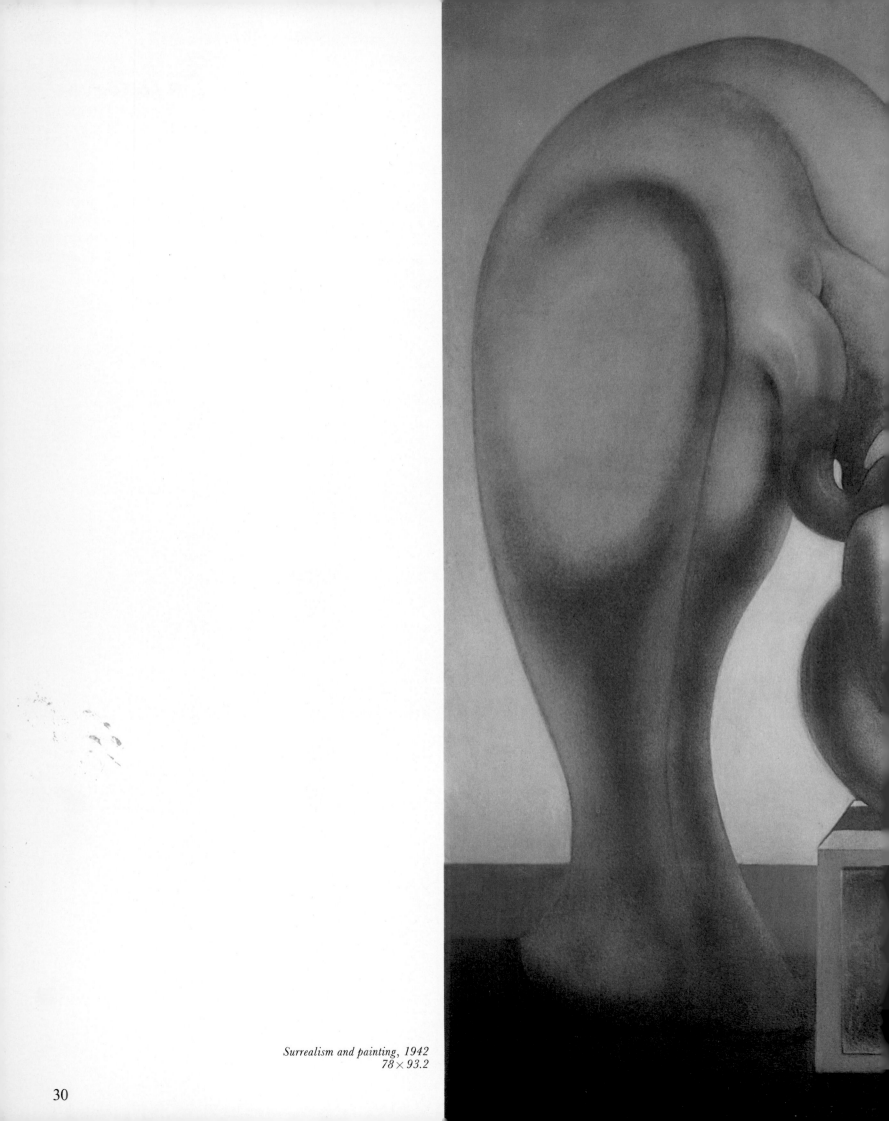

Surrealism and painting, 1942
78 × 93.2

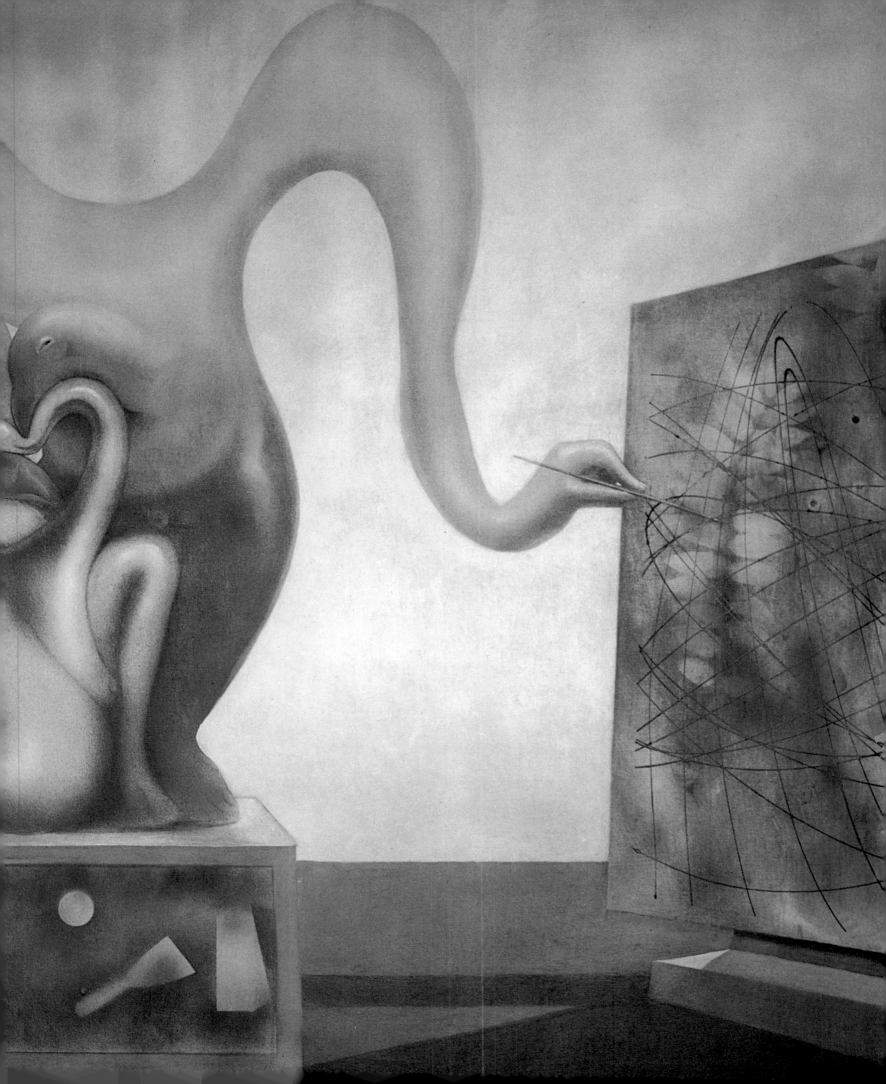

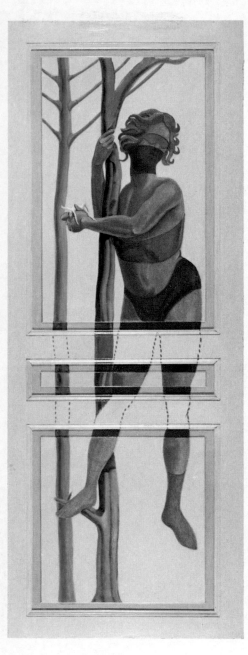

Going in coming out, 1923
80 × 32

As soon as Max Ernst began to paint, while a student at the University of Bonn, he invested in that activity all the resources of a sensitivity which experienced, to a point that was almost vertigo, whatever was disturbing about the outside world. His temperament led him to discover aspects of existence which many men do not even suspect. His childhood visions, while in a state of waking sleep, partook of genuine hallucinations. He has told, himself, how he distinctly saw, coming from the end of his bedroom, a cortege of men and women who passed by on either side of his bed; all he had to do was lean to the left or the right to see the faces of these apparitions. Later, in his reading, his strolls, his friendships, he looked for ways of giving perfect expression to his gifts of imagination and observation. One of his favorite painters was Caspar-David Friedrich, the German romantic whose tormented landscapes haunted him unceasingly. He was an assiduous reader of Nietzsche and Max Stirner, the great philosopher of anarchy. He frequented the *Young Rhineland* group, whose basic tenet was the necessity of transforming the fundamentals of poetry and painting.

Already, in his early youth, Max Ernst had emerged as a dandy and a rebel opposed to his family, upholding the rights of the individual against society, attacking all social conventions which cramped human freedom even ever so slightly. The world and its institutions, nature and its organic laws — together, he felt, they formed a set of permanent threats that had to be warded off. He found that painting, of the type accepted at that time, was too finicky and affected to denounce the deceptiveness of appearances and translate the horrors and delights of the inner

Vox Angelica, 1943
30.4 × 40.6

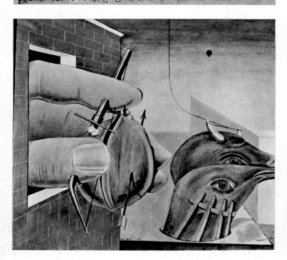

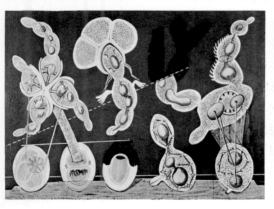

Poem-painting, 1923
26 × 20.8

Seashell, 1927
10.8 × 8.8

Oedipus Rex, 1922
41.2 × 37.6

Celebes the elephant, 1921
52 × 44

Selfportrait, 1909
7.2 × 4.8

Eislandschaften, Eiszapfen und
Gesteinsarten des weiblichen Körpers, 1920
(Landscapes of ice, icicles and minerals
of the female body)
Collage, pencil, gouache, 10.2 × 9.6

Chimeras, 1927
40 × 32.4

The graminaceous bicycle, 1920
Collage and gouache, 29.7 × 40

Fishbone forest, 1926
15.2 × 18.4

life, so he took up his position at the antipodes of painting, pending the moment when painting would have shed its futile prettiness. The disgust he felt at those who submitted to the established order of things led him to dadaism. Dada could be summed up in a single word, which the members of the movement strove to surpass each other in using: demoralization. The Dadaists' goal was to demoralize the public by destroying its so-called spiritual, so-called artistic, so-called social values. Max Ernst emitted some surprising flashes in this subversive undertaking with a series of explosive works — his collages and assemblages, trucelessly celebrating, like his engravings and paintings, the nonsense of the absurd.

But his genius was to vent itself still better in the broader context of surrealism than in the Dadaist framework. The surrealists' intention was not to destroy everything but to change everything under the spell of all that was marvelous. His intense imagination, his humor, his philosophical culture endowed Max Ernst with exceptional powers to make a lyrical and appealing world of phantasm spring forth from day-by-day reality. His best friend and accomplice was Paul Eluard, who bought his first pictures (he owned *Celebes the Elephant* and *Oedipus Rex*, among others) and wrote *Malheurs des Immortels* (Woes of the Immortals) with him. In 1923, living under Eluard's wing at Saint-Brice, in the forest of Montmorency, Max Ernst decorated his house with bizarre frescoes which, it is now agreed, were the starting point of his surrealist imagery. From that point on, Max Ernst was indeed the illustrator of the most secret dreams and desires, the revealer of the phenomena of the unconscious.

In the two decades between world wars, Max Ernst pursued a multi-form interpretation of the anxiety that grips modern man perceiving the multiple menaces of the universe. The result was a series of dramatic, violent images, haunted by the terrors and greed engendered by repressed instincts. His obsessions gave birth to persistent symbolic themes: theme of the eye identified with a star or a wheel, theme of the dark and inhospitable forest, theme of horses affronting a mare called "the bride of the wind," and above all, theme of the bird and everything having to do with birds, cages and eggs. Max Ernst's passion for birds, originating in childhood and nourished by reveries and reflection, led him to look on himself as a bird-man. Explaining his visions and aberrations, he has written, "I saw myself with the head of a kite-hawk and holding a knife in my hand, in the position of Rodin's *Thinker*". Physically, as those close to him have inevitably pointed out, he resembles a bird of prey. In his aggressiveness toward evil creatures, he is comparable to a bird of prey of which he is fond, the secretary bird, which

Fruit of long experience, 1919
Relief, 18.3 × 15.2

kills snakes by striking them with one of its wings while shielding itself with the other.

Max Ernst's painting during this first period was characterized by a two-fold determination: to describe anxiety, and to overcome anxiety. Describing anxiety was child's play for a visionary who read tragic scenes in the clouds, in the grain of wood. He brought forth a legion of monsters embodying the Spirit of Evil, like the *Domestic Angel* he shows us leaping in a sort of war dance. He denounced the upheavals of society and the disturbances of the human psyche. He showed that nature was not a soothing place of refuge and depicted it in terms of impenetrable forests, petrified cities, landscapes oppressed by a ring-like sun or moon. For the viewer's contemplation he offered jungles where terrifying fauna pullulated in a plethora of tangled vegetation; each plant, with wide, spear-shaped leaves, seemed as dangerous as the venomous creature it sheltered. Fishbone-flowers, animated minerals were ready to bruise one's flesh. The theme of carnivorous, man-eating, object-crushing nature culminated in the series of *Gardens that gobble airplanes*, which implied that everything was nothing but a trap. The enigmatic façades of the *Entire City*, the trees and vines of the *Déjeuner sur l'Herbe*, the gemlike formations of *Europe after the rain* were the fabulous decors in which he enclosed the drama of our time. The explanation and the outcome of this epic progression was *Vox Angelica;* the various compartments of this painting are so many windows opened onto other worlds. We are made to understand that those worlds belong to the inner as well as to the outer reality.

As for overcoming anxiety, Max Ernst proved that this was possible through use of a weapon he knew how to wield better than anyone else: grim humor. Laughter was crouching surreptitiously behind these images of terror, a sarcastic laugh which flouted convention, thwarted conformism, challenged emotion itself. A grave and scathing comic force, of almost painful intensity, emerges from the acute contrasts which he manages to establish — for instance, by taking an impassioned conflict to the utmost limit, by adding a preposterous detail to a gathering of serious figures, or by tossing an erotic element into the decor where you are least expecting it. Often, a bantering or impertinent title, poetic in a paradoxical way, dispels the feeling of despair which the scene exudes. It is somewhere around 1942 that the most profound mutation takes place in his work; this is when he paints *Surrealism and painting*, which places his own aims in doubt. It is a trip to the confines of a frightening country and it is made without fear, defiantly, brandishing the exorcisor's formula. Max Ernst refuses to be intimidated by negative forces. He teaches us to dominate whatever runs counter to the true life.

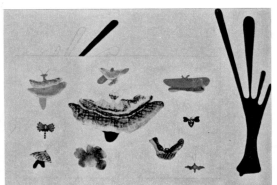

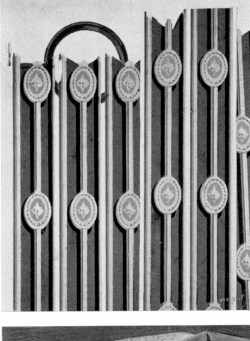

Kampf der Fische, 1917
(War of the Fishes)
Watercolor, 8.8 × 5.8

Schmetterlingssammlung, 1930-31
(Butterflies)
Collage with oil, India ink and pencil
on paper, 17.6 × 12

Inside eyesight, 1930. 40 × 32

Two children are threatened by a nightingale,
1924
Oil on wood, with wooden construction
and frame, 17.6 × 13.2

Forest and sun, 1922
Collage and gouache on cardboard 17.2 × 13.6

Garden that gobbles airplanes, 1935
Watercolor, 16 × 20

Red seascape, 1928
21.6 × 26

Anthropomorphical figure and seashell flower
(Loplop offers a flower), 1931
Oil and collage on plywood, 40 × 32.4

Pietà, or Revolution by night, 1923
46.4 × 35.6

IRRITATION OF THE VISIONARY FACULTIES

Prometheus, 1929
Collage from Femme 100 Têtes

COLLAGES

Max Ernst is generally considered the inventor of the collage. The cubists' papiers collés could not be compared to his creations because the intention behind them was not the same. When Braque or Juan Gris pasted a scrap of newspaper on a picture, they claimed to be grafting a chunk of raw reality onto painting. Max Ernst, on the contrary, wanted to use the most commonly met-with reality to create the effect of unfamiliarity. In 1919, in a city on the Rhine, he was leafing through an engineering catalogue when he suddenly realized what could be achieved by cutting out and mixing up the pictures. In this way the illustration type of collage was born. Ernst laid down the rules for this cunning game: figures and objects which, a priori, had nothing to do with one another, were brought together on the most unexpected level, the "level of non-suitability". From this encounter sprang mystery and surprise. To carry out this operation perfectly, one must not use strange or peculiar illustrations but rather starkly accurate, didactic ones. Ernst used magazines for this purpose as well as engraved plates taken from popular novels. By combining them, he forced the spectator to see what was strange in what was merely ordinary. Max Ernst is not a painter who shows the invisible. He shows what is hidden in what is visible. By 1929 Max Ernst had created a great variety of separate collages. Then it occurred to him to compose an entire novel in the same way — and the result was the *Femme 100 Têtes (100-Headed Woman)*, a magnificent picture album which he completed in two weeks, while sick in bed. The heroine, "Perturbation, my sister, the 100-headed woman", beautiful and nude as a statue, or clothed like a fashionplate striking scandalous poses, is shown in the most divers situations. She represents Rebellion, which has a hundred different faces. The hero is "Loplop", the "Superior of the Birds", spreading panic everywhere in order to please his mistress Perturbation. There is nothing accidental about the fact that one of the episodes in this story is entitled, "Fantômas, Dante and Jules Verne". Here we have a sort of Divine Comedy set out in the images of popular novels and horror films — a plunge into the unconscious, down to the source of hidden desires where latent conflicts show up in dreams or phantasmas where imagination triumphs over servitudes and frustration through inventions that exalt freedom.

THE 100-HEADED WOMAN

Loplop and the mouse's horoscope

*You can see more than one notary running away, rhythmically
dropping his voice*

Perturbation, my sister, the 100-headed woman

COLLAGES

Max Ernst continually improved the art of collage to a point where it became a mode of expression that was not subject to fluctuations. He assigned to it the power of revealing the secret dispositions of morals and the mind, and went so far as to state, "A collage is a hypersensitive and undeviatingly accurate instrument, like a seismograph, able to record the exact quantity of possibilities for human happiness at any given time". In 1933, he began a new collage-novel, for which he used a batch of cut-out pictures he had brought along in a suitcase. Three weeks later, he had put together *Une Semaine de Bonté, ou les Sept Eléments capitaux (A Week of Goodness, or the Seven Capital Elements)*, a more complex work than the *100-Headed Woman*, filled with more symbolical intentions.

It is a mythological cycle divided into seven phases, each illustrative of a specific theme. In the first phase, "Le Lion de Belfort" (The Lion of Belfort), we witness the misdeeds of a lion with a man's body, dressed by turns as an officer, a jailer, a streetporter, a bishop, or a lawyer, and decorated now with the Order of Agricultural Merit, now with the medal of the French School of Hairdressing. We see the lion-man throw a passerby over a parapet, assassinate passengers in a train compartment, throw himself upon a naked odalisk and devour one of her breasts, tickle the feet of a cadaver, beat a woman with his cane, shoot another dead with a revolver. He is led to the scaffold but takes the place of the executioner, whose severed head he offers to the crowd. Then he flees through a storm-blackened countryside and finally becomes a statue of a lion once again, raised on a billiard table. In the second part, "L'Eau" (Water), a woman is pitted against the aquatic element in all of its forms; she frolics with floods, tames the sea. The next series is "La Cour du Dragon" (Dragon's Courtyard), where reptiles and human figures with bats' wings frisk about; here there is a sublime image of Loplop, escorting a female guest, entering a salon where a monster lies convulsed on the floor. The sequences in the other chapters — "Oedipe", "Le Rire du Coq", "L'Ile de Pâques", "L'Intérieur de la Vue", "La Clé des Chants" (Oedipus, Cock's Laugh, Easter Island, Inside Eyesight, Key to Songs) — are no less swarming with hallucinating vicissitudes.

A Week of Goodness is an epic and grandiose work, both farcical and sinister, bursting with cruel lyricism. Its spectacle is an avenging universe, the scene of apparitions and prodigious feats where all rights go to the individual and the all-powerfulness of delirium in action is exalted. The pictures are of such quality that Goya's *Proverbs* come irresistibly to mind.

A
WEEK
OF
GOODNESS

FROTTAGES

Frottage (the technique of rubbing) was so important in Max Ernst's life that he spoke of it as solemnly as if it were a scientific discovery. Already, even before he had a revelation of what that technique could lead to, he had experimented with various things which were a limited application of it. In 1919, for a Dadist show in Berlin, he made some fifty drawings of combined or juxtaposed letters of the alphabet which he had reproduced by making graphite rubbings on paper of wooden block letters. But this was still a purely mechanical approach to frottage, somewhat like what children achieve by tracing over the contours of a coin. It was on August 10, 1925, in a hotel room in Pornic, that, wondering why the many grooves in the discolored floorboards held such facination for him, he placed a sheet of drawing paper on the floor and went over it with a lead pencil. Then he took this imprint and considered it from every possible angle until he hit upon the way it should be interpreted. A few pencil strokes were all that was needed to show what it suggested to him. In this first frottage, *Hugging the Walls*, we see a small branch behind a partition — the image which his copy of the floorboards caused to germinate in his mind. From then on, he used this process continually, placing his paper over all types of rough surfaces — a scrap of leather, a stale breadcrust, a piece of canvas sacking with raveled edges. Frottage became a method for investigating reality, the outcome of an interrogation of matter, a sort of soothsayer's device, in which the demon Analogy worked wonders. A frottage carried out on an oil painting on which Ernst used a comb to make wavy lines became a *Frost-Flower Shawl*. A frottage on a straw hat was to become the *Fascinating Cypress*. Another, over the thread unwound from a spool, evoked two gamboling horses, *The Stallion and the Bride of the Wind*.

A careful look at the thirty-four selected frottages which Max Ernst brought together in his *Natural History* proves that, in the alchemists' phrase, everything is in everything. The slightest thing contains a whole unknown world for whoever knows how to view it. An adventure of the mind can spring from the humblest object. And the painter, whom Ernst defines as a ''blind swimmer'', sees inside himself what reality screens from him.

Frottage from Natural History

The Marseillaise, 1931
Frottage on paper, 12.4 × 9.2

Fish, 1925
Frottage on paper, 13.2 × 18

Summertime, 1925
Frottage on paper, 8 × 10.5

Bertween the walls grow flowers, 1925
Frottage on paper, 8.3 × 6.4

Since earliest times, drawing and writing have grown apart and even become antagonistic. Most modern painters have tried to reconcile the two. Some of them, in order to make their strokes as eloquent as the letters of an alphabet, have taken their clues from Chinese calligraphy, others from Aztec pictography. The idea is that a drawing is no longer the stylized representation of a thing but the invention of a sign evoking an idea or creating a state of surprise in the beholder. Always, in his drawings, Max Ernst has aimed to increase the effectiveness of graphic language. In *Maximiliana*, he carried his possibilities to the highest degree, by producing entire pages of figurative writing. He was striving to write drawing, just as the ancient calligraphers strove to draw writing.

Maximiliana, or the Illegal Practice of Astronomy, is a series of plates which Max Ernst engraved in homage to an amateur 19th century astronomer, Guillaume Tempel, whom the official astronomers of his day challenged. Although a German, Tempel had a vagabond career; after living in Marseilles for nine years, he moved on to Milan and eventually died in Florence, where he was connected with the Arcetri observatory. He discovered the nebula of Merope in the Pleiades as well as the planet Angelina, and made several meteorological observations which remained unpublished. His great claim to glory was the discovery of the planet Maximiliana on March 8, 1861; the German astronomers later renamed it Cybele. Tempel accused the meteorologists of having un-learned to use their eyes. And precisely because Max Ernst wished to safeguard the future of vision, and establish a doctrine of the art of seeing, he recognized in Tempel an obscure brother deserving to be honored.

In order to compose *Maximiliana*, Max Ernst invented a type of writing which, apparently made up of runes and hieroglyphics, is so rich and so varied that not even the shrewdest persons can decipher it. He dared himself to use a language which never designates the same thing twice by the same word. Not one sign among this constellation of signs has a form comparable to the form of any other: a sovereign way of proving to us that speaking, writing, drawing —in a word, self-expression— should gush from one inexhaustible fantasy.

MAXIMILIANA

BEYOND PAINTING

*Head of a man intrigued by the flight
of a non-Euclidean fly, 1947
Oil on canvas, 35.2 × 26.4*

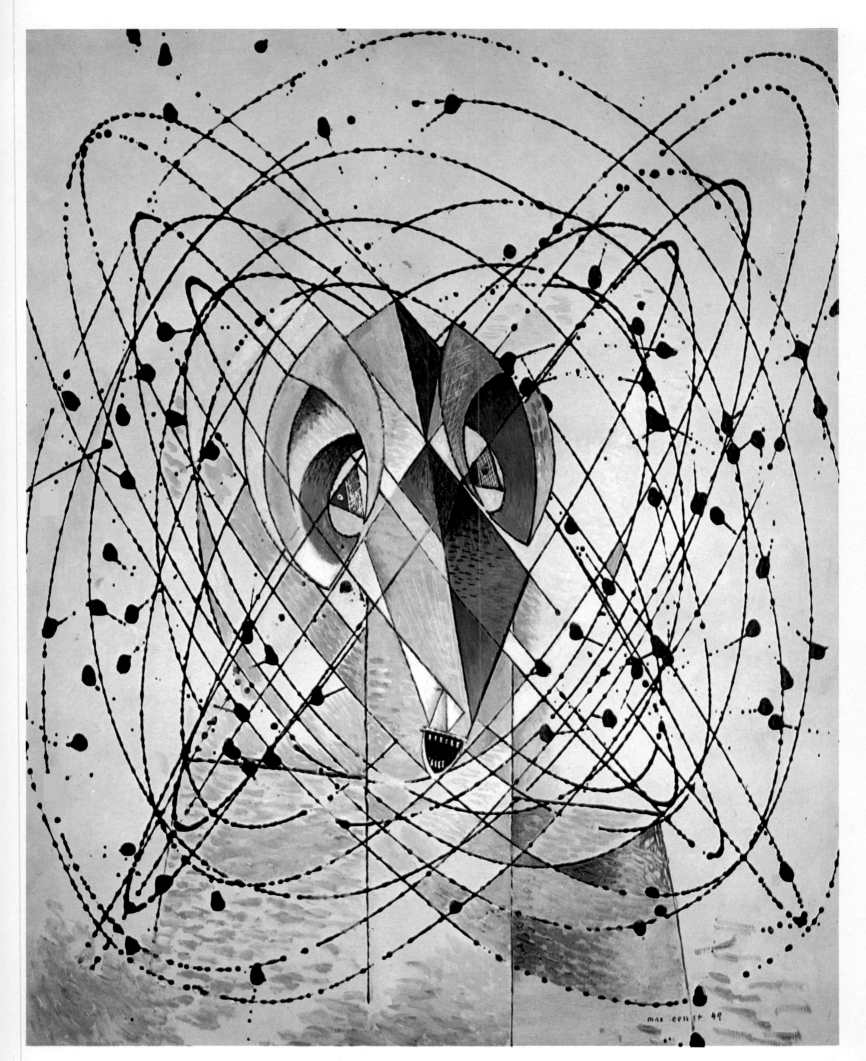

Design in nature, 1947
20.3 × 26.7

Die Geburt der Komödie, 1947
(The birth of comedy)
21.2 × 16

The cocktail-drinker, 1945
46.4 × 29

Euclid, 1945
26.2 × 23

Following two-page illustration: The palette, 1953
(detail), 35.6 × 46.4

51

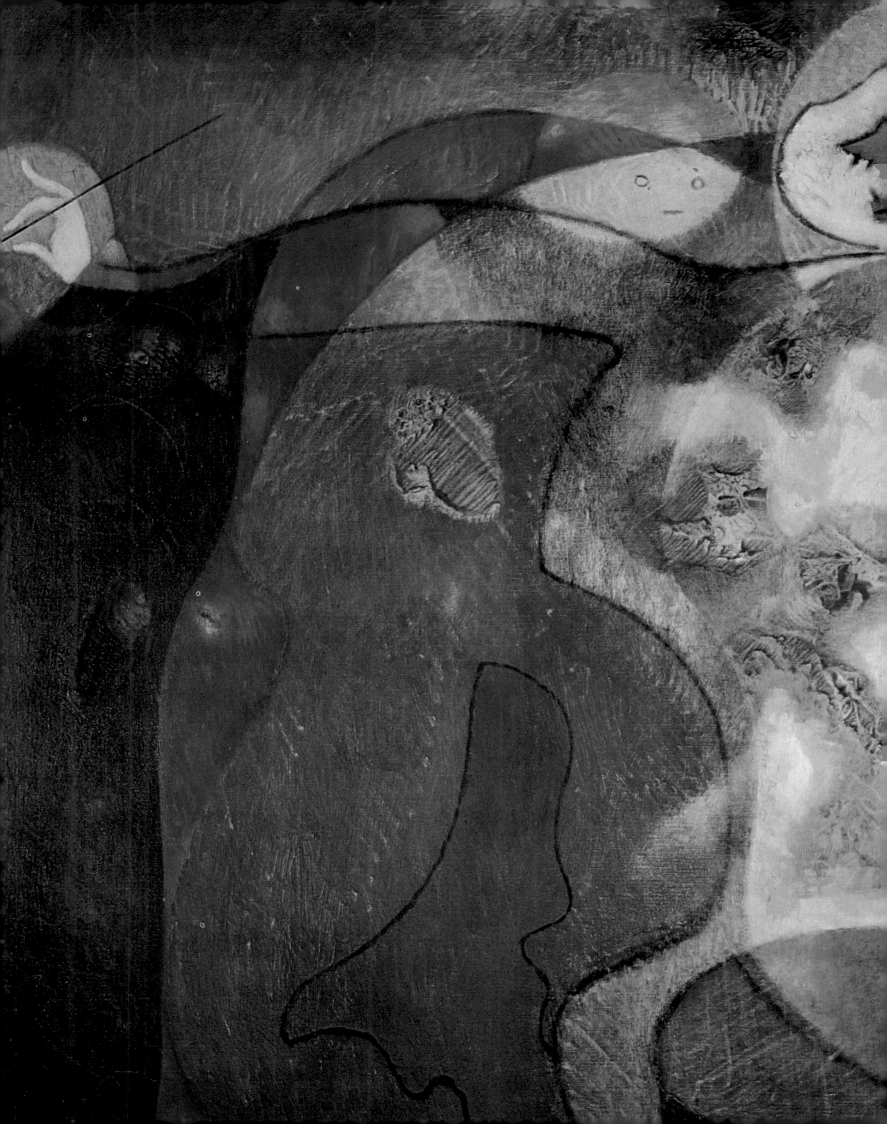

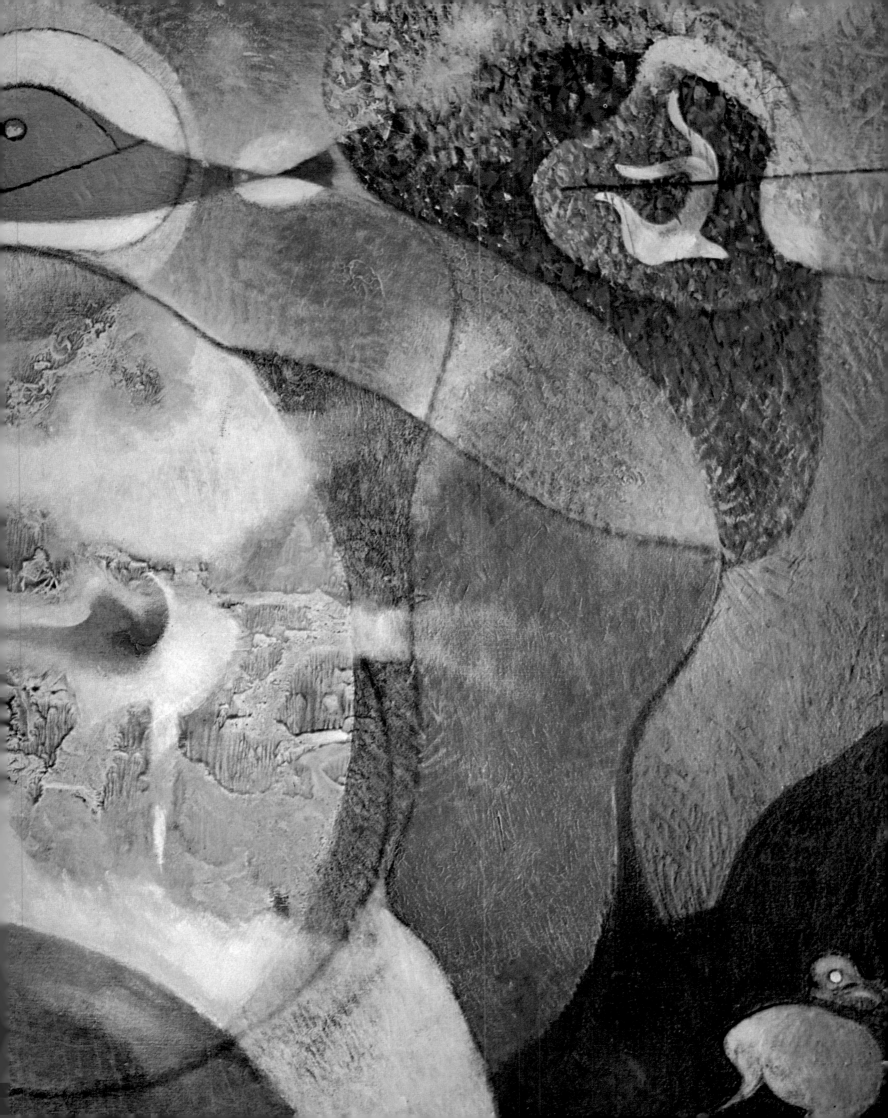

Bird, 1957
16.4 × 12

Two cardinal points, 1950
40.3 × 26.2

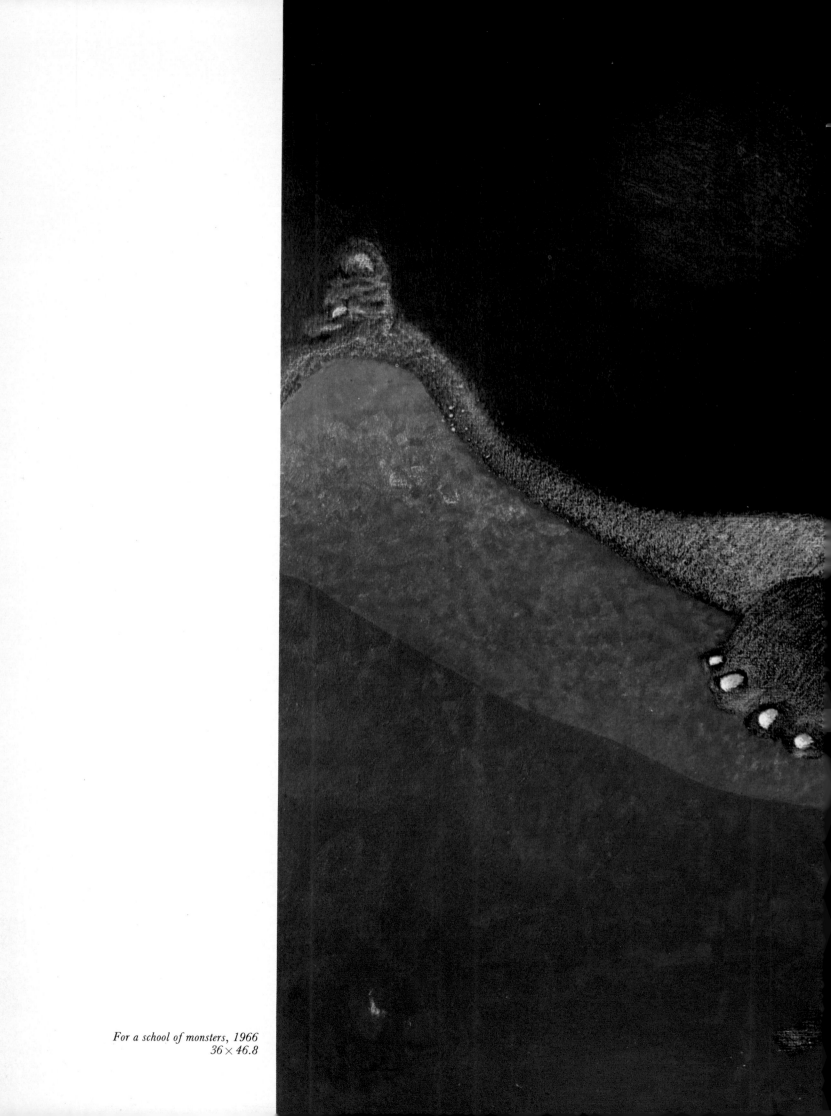

For a school of monsters, 1966
36 × 46.8

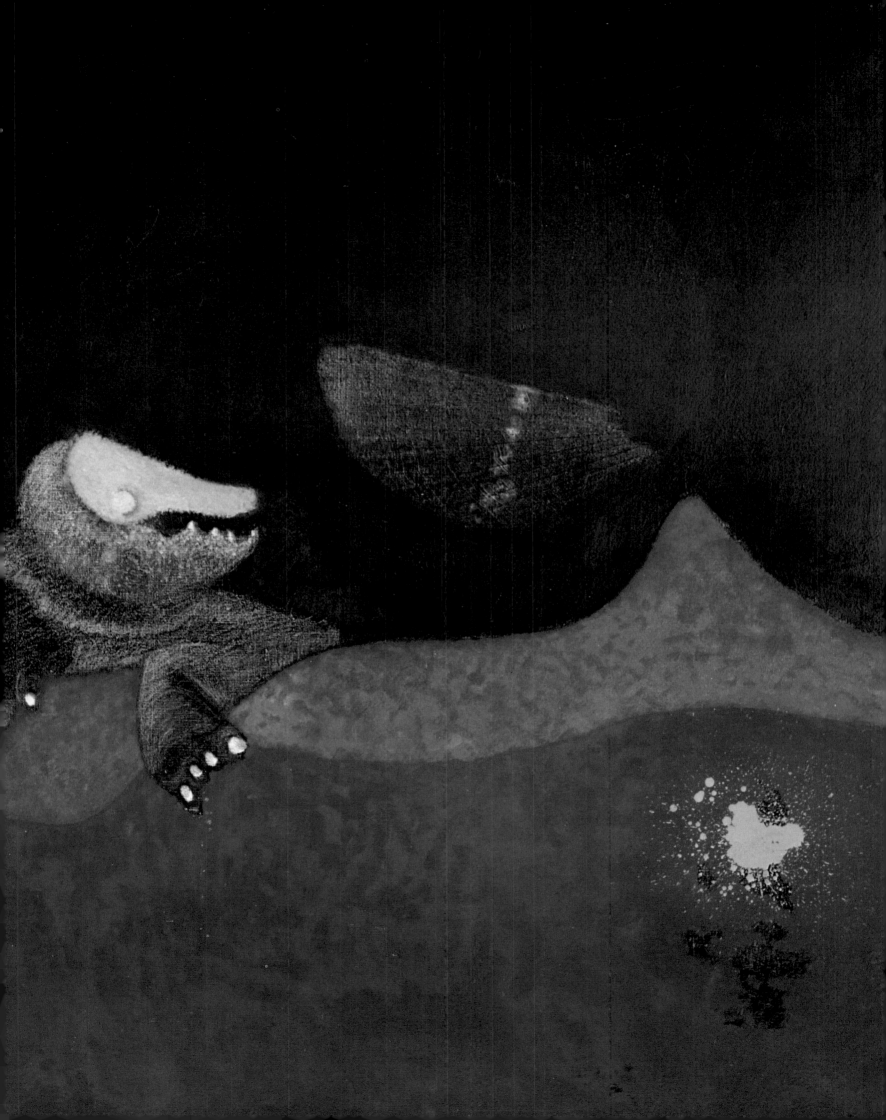

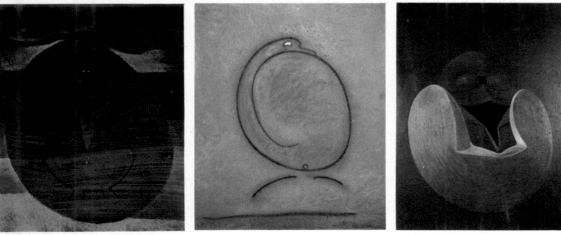

Fragezeichen, 1946
(Question mark)
13.2 × 9.6

Evangeline, 1957
26 × 21.

All in one
15.6 × 12.8

Back-flash, 1950
46.4 × 35.6

Springtime in Paris, 1950
46.4 × 35.6

Red Arizona, 1955
10.8×14

Blue Arizona, 1955
16.4×13.2

60

The Polish rider, 1954
46.4 × 35.6

Red forest, 1956
26.2 × 32.4

Tomb of the poet (After me, sleep), 1958
26 × 21.6

Microbes, 1947-53
Shown actual size

64

After the Second World War, there was a total renewal in Max Ernst's painting. During his stay in the United States, from 1941 to 1953, he exhausted all of the possibilities which he had inaugurated until then. With his *Head of a Man Intrigued by the Flight of a Non-Euclidean Fly*, done by laying the canvas flat on the ground, making a hole in a box filled with liquid paint and letting the box oscillate above the canvas, he continued to explore the techniques making it possible to "read the world" through the effects produced by chance. His large decalcomania works — *The Eye of Silence*, *The Stolen Mirror*, *Rhenish Night* — broadened his visionary universe. The paintings done in Arizona were a continuation of the cycle of phantomist landscapes. *Euclid* and *The Cocktail Drinker* were further portraits of disturbing heroes, possessed by the demons of knowledge or desire. But no sooner did he return to France than his personality underwent a metamorphosis. The man who had tackled painting with so much irony now gave himself over to the pleasure of painting. Was it because, after having been for so long appreciated only by a circle of avant-garde amateurs, the painter was now receiving virtually universal recognition? Or because, on the threshold of old age, he had a penchant for serenity? He now began to lavish tenderness upon his pictures, give them colors and matter, imbue them with an overall spirit that was no longer the expression of rebellion and challenge. Lights went on in his painting and grew brighter, inviting the beholder to a celebration of dazzling gaiety. Even so, this iridescence must not be taken quite at face value: just as all the joy of living and the intoxication of creativity were concealed behind the most terrifying images of his dark period, so a sort of luminous pessimism lurks beneath the radiant productions of his light period.

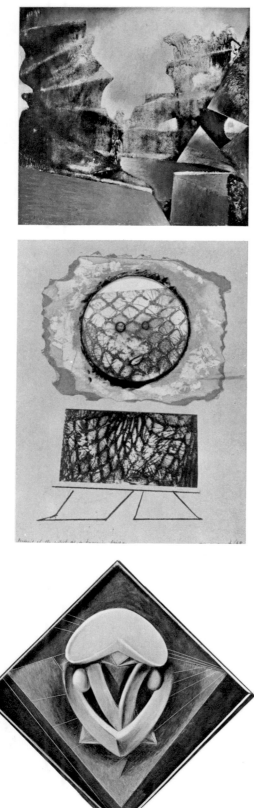

An enchanted conception of nature, heralded by certain landscapes painted in Arizona, filled him with contagious enthusiasm.
In 1953, he launched into the career of an out-and-out colorist.
Blue mountain and yellow sky, yellow sea and blue sun, birds
and oceans — it was relationships like these that he took pleasure in harmonizing in order to extol the intimate marriage of
sky and earth. He strove to express the wonderment that things
inspired in him. A trip to the country of his birth, for instance,
led to a painting of the Rhine, which is represented as a verti-
cal force — a veritable portrait of the river. When he settled in
Huismes, he was moved to capture the shimmering reflections
of the air in the Touraine region. His move to Seillans, in the
Var, opened him up to the warmth of the Midi. The joyous
transports of a holiday celebration in Seillans become a mosaic
of ecstatic faces. Orange-picking, in a large canvas called *A Tissue
of Lies*, is a flutter of masks, birds, golden balls on a background
of blue and green and yellow.

The unity of his work remained intact, and his initial quest
went on, stamped with the seal of absolute originality. Not only
did he revive the figures of his old mythology and continue to
contrive collages whose refinement revealed his sense of luxury,
but also he undertook to sing the praises of light in his own way.
He may paint an underwater background like a sky with a
sun radiating from the center, among the fish, or on the contrary, a sky like a sea tossed by squalls or small waves. Better
still, he creates a poetic confusion between mind and matter,
so that his landscapes seem to be not so much visions of
the outside world as reports on psychic life. As a result, we
are placed, as the title of one of his paintings puts it, "inside
eyesight".

The pattern of Max Ernst's development fits the principle of
contradiction he revered in his youth: having been the hero of
anti-painting in the days when painting was subject to retrograde
conventions, he became a lover of painting just as anti-painting
had become accepted to the point where it sometimes degene-
rated into academic pretention. *A Reasonable Earthquake*: this is
the title of one of his paintings and also the comparison which
his own personality brings to mind. He has wanted to be taken
for a nonchalant cataclysm, not the kind that creates havoc
and leaves only rubble behind, but one that is content merely
to shift the furniture around and arrange things in a different
order. In the eyes of posterity, Max Ernst will always be the
man who made painting tremble and quake; but whereas an
earthquake destroys everything, this artquake opened buds into
blossoming new forms.

Arizona landscape, 1953

Portrait of the artist as a human being, 1968
11.6 × 15.6

Head, 1948
21.6 × 21.6

Beatles, 1969
44.8 × 30.4

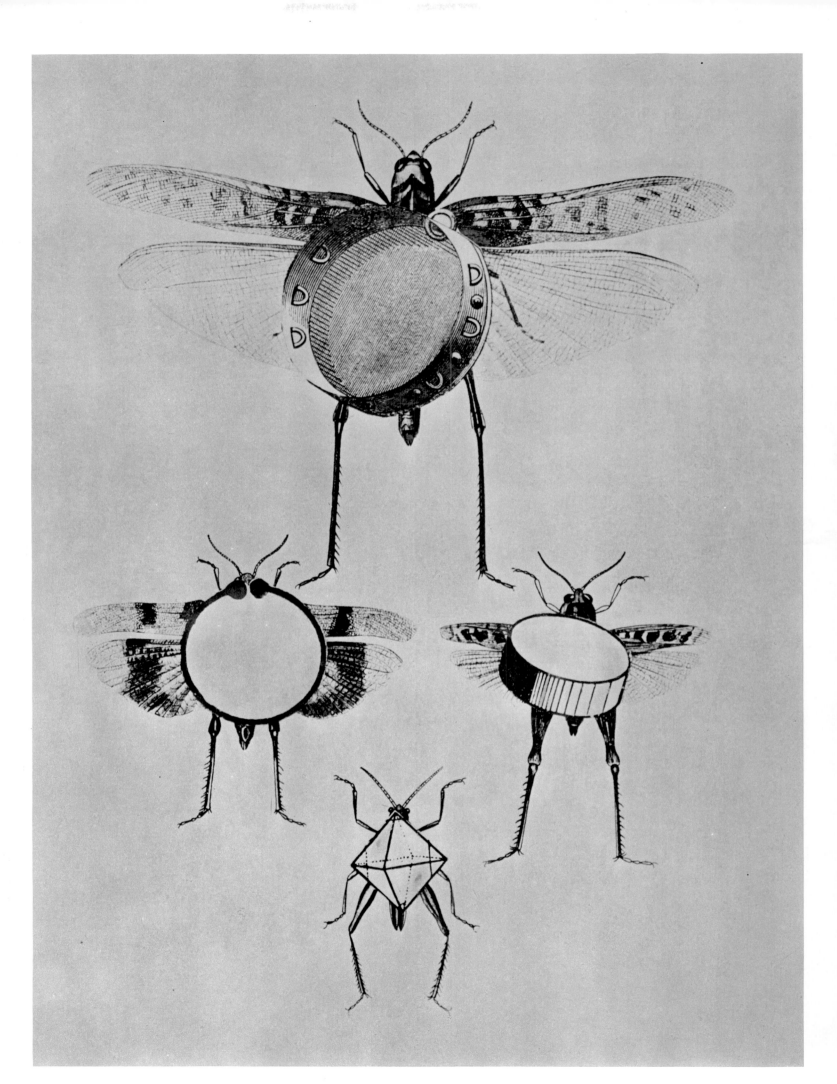

Mooring post, 1959
Bronze; height: 24.4

THE SCULPTURES

Max Ernst took up sculpture in order to materialize his dreams. It sometimes happens that a painter turns sculptor toward the end of his career, once his pictorial development has reached its ultimate stage. In so doing, he is seeking self-renewal either by exteriorizing in space the two-dimensional figures of his paintings or by trying out themes which he can later incorporate into his painting. But this was not the case with Max Ernst, who began to sculpt at the same time as he began to paint. In fact his first sculpture, *The Lovers*, of limewood picked out with gold, was done in Brühl in 1913. During his dadaist period in Cologne, he created assemblages using various materials, such as the *Dad'art object*, executed in 1919. But it was not until 1934 that he undertook a new series of plaster studies, including *Oedipus, The Beautiful Germanwoman, Moon Asparagus*, which were the prelude to such delicious inventions as the birdhead, the woman in the shape of a flower — surprising hybrids which spring from an imagination that is constantly on the alert.

The sculptures of Max Ernst correspond to a need to people daily life with familiar geniuses and modern deities. He has always thought of them as a guard of honor standing around him or as idols safeguarding his friends. In the course of one summer which he spent in Giacometti's home in Switzerland, he went out to get blocks of granite from a stream, shaped them and colored them, then scattered them throughout his host's garden. In 1938, he withdrew to a house at Saint-Martin-d'Ardèche, in France, which he decorated with reinforced concrete bas-reliefs; the wealth of animals that are depicted in them rivals the carvings over Gothic church doors. His home in Sedona, Arizona, was defended by his most impressive sculpture, *Capricorn*, showing a goat-headed god seated on a throne, with his zoomorphic female companion standing at his side. Such an extraordinary couple, stationed outside the house, was fit to shield it from the hostile forces of the desert and mankind. And in the last analysis, all of Max Ernst's sculptures look like chess pieces, enlarged and reinvented to suit his own purposes. For him, a statue is not a work of art but a work of play, a supreme entertainment in which fate has fun.

Capricorn, 1948-64
Bronze; height: 96; width: 82; thickness: 52

69

BIOGRAPHY

Max Ernst and Dorothea Tanning

1891: Max Ernst is born in Brühl, in the Rhineland, the second of six children, four girls and two boys. His father, Philippe Ernst, teaches in a school for the deaf and dumb.

1897-1908: goes to public school, graduates from the Brühl high school.

1909-1914: philosophy student at the University of Bonn.

1914-1918: drafted into the artillery during the war; does some watercolors in his spare time.

1919: With Arp and J. T. Baargeld, leads dadaist efforts in Cologne. Founds the Centrale Dada W/3, joined by the *Ouest-Stupidia* group, and organizes the first Dada show in Cologne.

1920: With Arp, composes collages which they dub *Fatagaga* (short for "FAbrique de TAbleaux GArantis GAzométriques", Factory of Authentically Gasometric Paintings). The Max Ernst show in Paris, in May, supported by a demonstration by Parisian dadaists, causes a sensation.

1921: Paul Eluard pays a visit to him in Cologne. It is the start of a friendship which will never flag.

1922: Takes part in a dadaist meeting in the Tyrol. With Eluard, writes *Woes of the Immortals*, prose poems which he also illustrates. Moves to Paris and paints *Friends' Rendez-vous*, an evocation of the future surrealists.

1923: To earn a living, designs cheap bracelets and cigarette holders for a souvenir factory.

1924: Travels in Indochina for several months with Paul Eluard, whom he joins in Singapore and accompanies to Saigon. Back in Paris, rallies to surrealism; André Breton has just published its *Manifesto*.

1925: Discovers frottage.

1926: With Miró, creates the décors and costumes for *Romeo and Juliet*, performed by the Diaghilev ballet troupe.

1927: Marries Marie-Berthe Aurenche.

1929: Publishes the *100-Headed Woman*. Beginning of his friendship with Giacometti.

1930: Bunuel and Dali give him a part in their film, *L'Age d'Or*.

1931: Has his first show in New York, at the Julien Levy gallery.

1933: Is placed on the Nazis' black list.

1934: Publishes *A Week of Goodness*. While spending the summer at Giacometti's house in Maloja, Switzerland, decorates the garden of it with carved blocks of granite.

1936: Starts work on some large paintings, using the decalcomania (transfer) process. Exhibits 48 paintings at the "Fantastic art, Dada and Surrealism" show held at the Museum of Modern Art in New York.

1937: Does the décors for *Ubu enchaîné* at the Comédie des Champs-Elysées in Paris.

1938: Breaks temporarily with the surrealist group. In the company of Leonora Carrington, withdraws to a house in Saint-Martin-d'Ardèche.

1939-40: Interned as a foreigner in various concentration camps in southern France.

1941: Leaves France for the United States. Stays in California. Marries Peggy Guggenheim. Is reconciled with Breton, takes part in the activities of the exiled surrealists.

1942: Meets Dorothea Tanning.

1943: Learns of his father's death. Travels in Arizona.

1944: Works on a series of sculptures. Spends the summer on Long Island.

1945: Wins a painting competition on the subject of *The Temptation of Saint Anthony*.

1946: Marries Dorothea Tanning. Builds a wooden house in Sedona, Arizona.

1949: Sails back to Europe from New Orleans.

1950: First retrospective show, at the Galérie Drouin in Paris.

1951: Retrospective at Brühl castle, in his native city.

1952: Lectures at the University of Honolulu while traveling in the Hawaiian Islands.

1953: Returns to Paris. Retrospective at Knokke-le-Zoute. Goes to Cologne in search of the ghosts of his youth.

1954: Grand Prix of the Venice Biennale. Is excluded from the surrealist group.

1955: Settles on a farm, "Le Pin perdu", at Huismes, in the Touraine.

1956: Retrospective at the Kunsthalle in Berne.

1958: Becomes a French citizen. Publication of Patrick Waldberg's *Max Ernst* (J-J. Pauvert, Paris, ed.).

1959: Retrospective at the Musée national d'art moderne in Paris.

1960: Series of paintings entitled *The Aeolian Harp*, where the bars of a bird cage are identified with the strings of a harp.

1961: Retrospective at the Museum of Modern Art in New York. The city of Cologne awards him its Stefan Lochner medal.

1962-1965: Series of important exhibitions at the Tate Gallery in London, the Walraf-Richartz-Museum in Cologne, the Kunsthaus in Zurich, the Grimaldi museum in Antibes, and the Galerie Alexander Iolas in Paris.

1966: "Beyond painting" exhibition at the Palazzo Grassi in Venice.

1968: Inauguration of the Fontaine d'Amboise, sculpture by Max Ernst.

1971: Retrospective at the Orangerie of the Louvre in Paris.

BIBLIOGRAPHY

I. BOOKS BY MAX ERNST

Fiat Modes. Album of 8 lithographs. Cologne, Schlomilch Verlag, 1919.

Les Malheurs des Immortels (Woes of the Immortals) revealed by Paul Eluard and Max Ernst. Prose poems written by Eluard and Ernst together, and illustrated by twenty-one collages by Ernst. Paris, Librairie Six, 1922.

Histoire naturelle (Natural History). 34 plates, prefaced by Jean Arp. Paris, Jeanne Bucher, 1926.

La Femme 100 Têtes (The 100-Headed Woman). Collage-novel. Note to the reader by André Breton. Paris, Editions du Carrefour, MCMXXIX.

Rêve d'une Petite Fille qui voulait entrer au Carmel (Dream of a Little Girl Who Wanted to Become a Carmelite Nun). Collage-novel. Paris, Editions du Carrefour, MCMXXX.

Une Semaine de Bonté ou les Sept Eléments capitaux (A Week of Goodness, or the Seven Capital Elements). Collage-novel. Paris, Jeanne Bucher, 1934.

Sept Microbes vus à travers un Tempérament (Seven Microbes Seen Through a Temperament). Paris, Editions Cercle des Arts, 1953.

Paramythen. Gedichte und Collagen (Stories and Collages). Cologne, Verlag Galerie Der Speigel, 1955.

Twelve Reproductions in Color. Foreword by Georges Bataille. Unpublished text by Max Ernst, Paris, Editions d'Art Gonthier-Seghers, 1960.

Maximiliana ou L'Exercice illégal de l'Astronomie (Maximiliana, or the Illegal Practice of Astronomy). Etchings and writings to illustrate and comment upon the findings of Guillaume Tempel, illumined by Iliazd. Paris, Le Degré Quarante-et-un, 1964.

Ecritures (Writings), Paris, Gallimard, Collection "Point du Jour", 1970.

II. BOOKS ABOUT MAX ERNST

Max Ernst. Works from 1919 to 1936. With a text by Max Ernst, "Au-delà de la peinture" and various comments on painting. Paris, Editions Cahiers d'Art, 1937.

Homage to Max Ernst, 2nd series, no. 1, April 1942. Special issue of *View* magazine devoted to Max Ernst.

Beyond Painting, and other writings by the artist and his friends. New York, Wittenborn, Schultz, Inc., 1948.

Max Ernst. Bousquet, Joe-Tapie, Michel. Paris, René Drouin, 1950.

Max Ernst. Waldberg, Patrick. Paris, Jean-Jacques Pauvert, 1958.

Max Ernst. Trier, Eduard. Recklinghausen, Verlag Aurel Bongers, 1959.

Max Ernst, Frottages. Spies, Werner. Translated into French by Andre Daniel, Paris, Pierre Tisné, s.d.

Max Ernst, Life and Work. Russell John. London, Thames and Hudson, and New York, Abrams, 1967.

Max Ernst chez Paul Eluard. Waldberg, Patrick. Paris, Galerie André-François Petit, Editions Denoël, 1969.

The photographs are by
Jean-Pierre Lebert, Walter
Dräyer, Paul Facchetti,
Usis, Jacqueline Hyde,
P. Hinous, Frederic Sommer, and X.

We wish to thank the collectors and museums who gave us their kind assistance, including: Mrs. Helene Anavi, Paulhiac; Mrs. Simone Collinet, Paris; Mr. and Mrs. Jean de Menil, Houston, Texas; Mr. Willian N. Copley, New York; Mr. M. H. Franke, Murrhardt; Mr. Wilhelm Hack, Cologne; Mr. Alexandre Iolas, Paris, New York; Mrs. Krebs, Brussels; Staatliche Kunsthalle, Karlsruhe; Kunsthaus, Zurich; Städt. Kunstsammlungen, Bonn; Kunstsammlung Nordrhein-Westfalen; Mr. Maurice Lefebvre-Foinet, Paris; Mr. Julien Levy, Bridgewater, Connecticut; Mrs. Edmée Maus, Geneva; Mr. A. D. Mouradian, Paris; Museum of Modern Art, New York; National Museum, Stockholm; Wallraf-Richartz Museum, Cologne; Mr. and Mrs. Günther Peill, Cologne; Mr. Francesco Pelizzi; Galerie Schwartz, Milan; Clemens Sels-Museum, Neuss; Galerie Tronche; Mr. J. B. Urvater, Rhode-Saint-Genèse; Wadworth Atheneum, Hartford, Connecticut; Mrs. Line Waldberg, Paris; Moderna Museet, Stockholm; Galerie Der Spiegel, Cologne; Messrs. Nesuhi and Ahmet Ertegun, New York; Mr. Werner Schindler, Zurich.

The measurements of all works illustrated in this volume are given in inches; height precedes width.